Blacq's Tastings

The Boug-Ghetto Chronicles

Ms. Blacq

authorHOUSE®

AuthorHouse™
1663 Liberty Drive
Bloomington, IN 47403
www.authorhouse.com
Phone: 1 (800) 839-8640

Published by AuthorHouse   04/29/2016

ISBN: 978-1-5246-0618-3 (sc)
ISBN: 978-1-5246-0617-6 (e)

Library of Congress Control Number: 2016906914

Print information available on the last page.

Any people depicted in stock imagery provided
by Thinkstock are models, and such images are
being used for illustrative purposes only.
Certain stock imagery © Thinkstock.

This book is printed on acid-free paper.

Because of the dynamic nature of the Internet, any web
addresses or links contained in this book may have changed
since publication and may no longer be valid. The views
expressed in this work are solely those of the author and
do not necessarily reflect the views of the publisher, and
the publisher hereby disclaims any responsibility for them.

Contents

Blacq's Cognac

Blacq's Intro

This book is something like a self-help book. kind of, the reason I say kind of is because no one is perfect! By no means am I writing this as if I have life all figured out! Just a girl with a talent of putting a few words together & making sense of them. The only thing that qualifies me to bring you these writing is the trails of life, love, & reality that I have face & conquered with grace & poise!

The purpose for these writings are to raise awareness and conciseness where the eye of the mind is asleep as well as allow people to know they are not alone. We have all done things we are not too proud of, lied, cheated, used as well as those things have been done to us. Some have been given a death sentence from the doctor. others have been abused mentally, physically, emotionally, & wants to break free, just doesn't know how. These writings are intended to give one an Aha moment, give encouragement, &

HOPE! IF YOU'VE EVER LOVED & DIDN'T RECEIVE THAT LOVE BACK THIS IS FOR YOU ALSO.

BLACQ'S TASTINGS IS COMPOSED OF THREE SECTIONS BLACQ'S LEMONADE, BLACQ'S TEA, & BLACQ'S COGNAC. THESE THREE SECTION REPRESENT TRIALS THAT ARE FACED IN LIFE, LOVE, & REALITY. A LOT OF TIMES WE WANT TO LIVE LIFE WITH ROSE COLORED SHADES ON, BUT FACT IS SHIT AIN'T ALWAYS BEAUTIFUL. THINGS CAN GET REAL UGLY REAL FAST. WHEN THIS HAPPENS, WHAT DO YOU DO? SOME GET DEPRESSED, SOME MASK AS IF THEY DON'T CARE, SOME REALLY DON'T CARE & OTHERS CARRY IT FOR A LIFETIME. GUESS WHAT, LIFE IS WAY TOO SHORT & BEAUTIFUL TO BE WASTING IT ON MISERY OR NONCHALANT TACTICS. I HOPE THIS HELPS SOMEONE IN SOME WAY. I CAN BE A LOT TO TAKE IN, SO YOU MIGHT WANT TO DO THIS AS A TASTING, IN SMALL DOSES MAYBE ONE READING AT A TIME. TO NOT GET OVERWHELMED BY THIS BOUG-GHETTO EDUCATIONAL TASTING. ENJOY THESE WRITINGS AS YOU DO THE DRINKS THEY ARE NAMED AFTER.

Blacq's Lemonade

Misconstrued

I am a misfit, a non-conformist, eccentric, abnormal some say I'm weird, I've been considered a rebel! Peculiar, anomalous, unusual, and strange! Misunderstood yet loyal. I am a square business, no-nonsense kind of gal! I am free. I am me. I am Success & most of all I have not finished yet! Other people's issues or hang-ups about me, don't mean anything. I've dealt with this since the day I was born. In the eyes of others uncomely & dark skinned automatically grouped me in. Grouped in with a bunch of negative stereo-types that literally had nothing to do with me. So I live and rise above it all; embracing me the wonderful and beautiful me! We are all uniquely made no mistakes in our creation took place. Let's talk about turning sour experiences sweet. Blacq's lemonade

YOU

Embrace you, your flaws, your perfections, your mistakes, your victories! Love those who love you, forgive those who wronged you. Hope for the very same in return. Love life, accomplish your goals, love the great creation of you! You deserve every bit of happiness coming your way.

Beautiful Reality

I tossed and turned all night. The dream I had was heart wrenching & real. I saw it once before it was true. Hurtful but very real & true! At the time it was My truth! How could one be so deceitful? In the midst of it all I realize there is absolutely nothing wrong with me. I deserve the best simply because I am the best. I exude greatness in each and every thing that I do. I'm fine & with time I'll be even better. Today I lift my head up and journey to a happier place; a place where my happiness & joy are reality.

Invisible Chains

Once there where chains placed physically on wrist and ankles, toting African people away, away to a place they would be forced to call home. Involuntarily taken from their homeland with extreme force. The men were emasculated, both physically and mentally. Minimized in front of their women and children. These acts were committed so the message would ring clear. Longing for a place once called home, most died by European disease or jumping ship into the sea. The ones that did arrive alive had been conditioned. The belief engrained was that their worth was that of a worker bee. Self-worth destroyed and minimized only to increase their owner's currency. Pummels, thrashings, and the rape of the African women. this consummation said; "you are here, you are now my property" and Forced to be an African American. Things were unambiguous and the intentions surly weren't eventual friendship. Two hundred years

OF INTENTIONAL OPPRESSION! EVENTUALLY THINGS
HAVE CHANGED, LAWS PUT IN PLACE AND DOORS ONCE
CLOSED, FLUNG OPEN. DECADES LATER, WE HOLD ON
TO THE INVISIBLE CHAINS. THESE CHAINS ARE NO
LONGER PHYSICAL BUT WRAPPED AROUND OUR MINDS.
LOVING THE GYRATIONS OF A NATION OF SUPPOSED
QUEENS. MOTHER EARTH HAS BEEN DECREASED TO
CHILD SUPPORT AND SINGLE MOTHERING. BLAMED BY
THE MEN THAT WERE ONCE FILLED WITH THE LUST OF
THEIR BOSOMS. WHO IS TO BLAME FOR THE LOVELESS
ENCOUNTER'S WHICH CAUSES THEIR FATHERHOOD
TO VANISH INTO THIN AIR. EQUATING THE VALUE
OF THEIR CHILDREN, THEIR VERY OWN FLESH AND
BLOOD TO THE WOMEN THEY NEVER LOVED. THIS
IS ACCEPTABLE IN OUR COMMUNITIES BECAUSE OF
TARNISHED AND DISTORTED MIND FRAMES OF THE
JIM CROW PROMISE. THE CYCLE GOES ON! BROKEN
HOME AFTER BROKEN HOME. INVISIBLE CHAINS
CAUSING ALL CIVILS RIGHTS LEADERS TO FLIP OVER IN
GRAVES. THEY THOUGHT THEY BROKE THE CHAINS
BUT IN REALITY PAVED THE WAY TO A FALSE SINCE OF
FREEDOM. RAPPERS RAP ABOUT GOLD CHAINS AND
BIG BOOTY STRIPPER WHORES. CAUSING LITTLE BOYS
IN MEN'S BODIES TO FLEE THEIR VOWS EXCHANGED.
SEARCHING FOR DIFFERENT TYPES OF SODOMY;
CHANGING THE BEAUTY OF WHAT IS SUPPOSED TO

HAPPEN ON A MARITAL BED. MOST ATHLETES MARRY CAUCASIAN SAYING A SISTER, ONE THAT RESEMBLES THE MOTHER HE HATES ISN'T WORTHY OF THE SPOTLIGHT. IN THEIR MIND WEALTH ACHIEVED IS FOR THE SOPHISTICATED. WHITE WASHED THEY BELIEVE AFRO PUFFS AND INDEPENDENCE SAY ANGER AND RAGE WHEN IN REALITY IT'S A CRY FROM THE QUEEN FOR THE KING TO HELP BREAK INVISIBLE CHAINS. CHAINS THAT WERE ONCE PHYSICAL, BUT NOW CHAINED TO OUR BRAINS.

PURSUIT

What's happiness?

Is it having lots of friends and money to spend?

Is it short days long nights?

Is it pussy, money and weed?

falling to sleep in the arms of that special someone or

Sailing the seven seas?

Eating whatever you please until you almost burst, but like magic no pounds gained?

Is it living life care free with zero fucks given?

Happiness for me is good looks, wealth, health, and prosperity.

& for you? What about you? Hey you, yeah you?

THE MORAL OF THE STORY IS FIND YOUR HAPPY PLACE!!!

DRIVE IN YOUR VERY OWN LANE & GUESS WHAT?!?!

THERE IS NO TRAFFIC THERE. IN YOUR LANE YOU CAN CHASE EVERY DREAM IMAGINABLE AT YOUR VERY OWN PACE AND SINCE IT'S YOUR LANE NO ONE ELSE'S OPINION MATTERS.

ARE YOU ON THE PURSUIT OF HAPPINESS OR ARE YOU JUST ALIVE UNTIL YOU DIE?

SELF-LOVE

ARE YOU ABSOLUTELY UNDENIABLY IN LOVE WITH YOU?

WHEN YOU SEE YOUR REFLECTION IN THE MIRROR ARE YOU ULTIMATELY PLEASED?

CAN YOU GO INTO A GROUP OF PEOPLE WITH NO HESITATIONS OR EXPLANATIONS?

YOUR WILDEST DREAMS DO YOU PLAN TO MAKE THEM COME TRUE?

THIS SMALL LIST OF QUESTIONS IS ALL ABOUT YOU.

NOT YOUR MOM AND WHAT SHE DID TO RUIN YOUR LIFE!

FORGET ABOUT YOUR DAD HE LEFT AND HAS TO FACE HIMSELF FOR THAT.

YOUR LIFE IS WHAT YOU MAKE IT & IT'S ALL ABOUT CHOICES!

LOVING YOURSELF LIMITLESSLY IS FREE &SHOULD BE DONE EVERY MOMENT OF EACH & EVERYDAY; LOVE YOU!

SAYS WHO?

STATUS QUO IS TREMENDOUSLY OVERRATED. TO BE BORN HUMAN IS TO BE RAISED A CERTAIN WAY. GO TO SCHOOL AT LEAST ACQUIRING A HIGH SCHOOL DIPLOMA AND DREAMS OF THE PERFECT HOURLY WAGE. GET MARRIED, SIGN FOR A THIRTY-YEAR MORTGAGE ADD A FEW KIDS AND LIVE THE AMERICAN DREAM. LIVING LIFE VICARIOUSLY THROUGH THE T.V. SCREEN. SEEMS RATHER BORING IF YOU ASK ME. LIVING LIFE SHOULD HAVE NO LIMITS. EAT DIFFERENT FOODS, TRAVELING, PET A LION, SPEAK WITH A HOMELESS PERSON, SPREAD YOUR ASHES ACROSS THE LAND. IT'S TOTALLY OKAY.

Reinvention

Hurt is a prevalent emotion in our world & is a very uncomfortable feeling. The beauty of any emotion or feeling is that in time they pass. When you are experiencing an unjust dissolution of any kind of relationship, remember it's not your fault. Things that happen aren't always fair, don't try to place a guilt trip on the opposing party, chances are if they trampled your love like a heard of horses, ask yourself do they really care? You must at that point take care of you. Feel that feeling as uncomfortable as it is, but keep in mind feelings change just as the other person's decision to love you changed, most time this happens with no closure involved. Closure is needed, however you can't force closure out of anyone. Move forward knowing that You deserve the very best & if you know you loved with no limits rest peacefully in that & begin to offer self-closure. Self-closure in this writing will be called reinvention. The days leading

UP TO YOUR REINVENTED SELF WILL BE HARD. WHEN YOU DECIDED TO REINVENT YOURSELF REALIZE THE PROCESS THAT MUST TAKE PLACE. RE-LOVING YOURSELF IS TOTALLY POSSIBLE & FACT IS IT'S THE BEST LOVE ON EARTH ONE COULD EVER RECEIVE. PICK UP A NEW HOBBY, READ A BOOK PREFERABLY A BLACQ BRAND EXCLUSIVE. CHANGE YOUR HAIR STYLE OR HAIRCUT. PICK A NEW COLOR POLISH AND NAIL LENGTH. BUY YOU A NEW SHIRT, TIE & EVEN MATCHING SOCKS. HURT IS NOT BIASED IT CAN HAPPEN TO ANYONE AT ANY TIME. YOU JUST HAVE TO FACE IT HEAD ON & NOT ALLOW IT TO VICTIMIZE YOU FOR TOO LONG. YOUR REINVENTION IS AWAITING YOU.

Cycle change

Being Dysfunctional is as common as a hand bag with matching shoes. Boy children are just as susceptible to molestation by males, as girl children are. Let's not leave out the fact that women do this to children both girls and boys as well. Double standards are okay in the workplace which is definitely discrimination but no one addresses it. People keep quit cause Retaliation is likely in place of justice. Children watch their parents mentally, emotionally & physically abuse one another, & the aggressor can be either mom or dad. Children have babies out of wedlock, trapping those children created in that act into poverty and cycles that no one speaks of breaking. Dark skin & curly hair may as well be a disability, while the owners are asked to be petted like animals in the local zoo. Minorities are told they should start at community colleges because they are not "smart" enough for universities, I mean unless of course they are athletic & then

ACCEPTED SINCE THEY WILL GO ON LIKE ONE IN BLACK FACE SUITED ONLY FOR PEOPLE'S ENTERTAINMENT. CHILDREN WITH A SMALL AMOUNT OF EXTRA ENERGY ARE LABELED AS HAVING ADHD. THE USAGE OF DRUGS DURING PREGNANCY IS NOT PUBLICLY ADDRESSED REGULARLY LIKE THE CONCERT OF A CELEBRITY COMING TO TOWN. THE DYSFUNCTIONAL CYCLE CONTINUES! HOW CAN YOU LOVE A CHILD YOU CARRY WHEN YOU WERE THE UNLOVED CHILD YOURSELF? LET'S FACE FACTS THE VALUE AND PURITY OF SELF WAS NEVER TAUGHT. YOUR MOM CALLED YOU NAMES AND POKED FUN AT YOUR SKIN, MAINLY BECAUSE SHE LOVED YOUR DAD BUT, HE BROKE HER HEART & THAT'S WHEN YOU BECAME THE HOUSEHOLD SIN. MIDDLE CHILD YOU'RE NOT THE OLDEST, EVERYONE FROM GRANDMA TO UNCLE'S STAR. NEITHER THE BABY TO BE PAMPERED AND CATERED TOO, NO NOT BY FAR. NO MATTER WHAT DYSFUNCTIONAL TENDENCY YOU WERE MADE ACCUSTOMED TO IN YOUR LIFE MAKE THE CONSCIOUS DECISION TO BREAK THE CYCLES; CYCLES THAT HAVE BEEN PASSED OFF AS NORMAL. THE BREAKING OF CYCLES IS A TASK, THEY ARE COMFORTABLE, FAMILIAR & HAVE CLAIMED YOU AS A VICTIM. YOU WERE MOLESTED, YOU WERE PICKED ON, YOU WERE DISOWNED, YOU WERE CALLED UGLY, YOU WERE TAUGHT ILLITERACY, YOUR DAD SPENT HIS LIFE IN JAIL, MOM WAS PROMISCUOUS,

YOU WERE BEAT YOU WITNESSED FAMILY VIOLENCE FROM PHYSICAL, MENTAL TO VERBAL ABUSE. IT'S OKAY BREAK THE CYCLES TODAY, SEEK HELP, GET COUNSELING. YOU CAN DO IT YOUR VICTORIOUS YOU ARE LOVED YOU ARE SPECIAL & YOU CAN LIVE A LIFE OF UNLIMITED ACCOMPLISHMENTS. HAPPINESS AND JOY IS YOUR DESTINY. START THE CYCLE OF CHANGE.

LOSE BULB

ONE OF MY FONDEST MEMORIES AS A YOUNG GIRL IS MY MOM'S FESTIVE WAYS; ESPECIALLY WHEN IT CAME TO DECORATING OUR FAMILY CHRISTMAS TREE. THE SEASON TO GIVE IN THE SMITH HOUSEHOLD ALWAYS CAME WITH THE OBSTACLES OF PULLING OUT LAST YEAR'S DECORATIONS AND FIGURING OUT WHICH STRING OF LIGHTS WORKED. ONE YEAR MY MOM WAS SICK, SO I DECIDED TO GET MY BROTHERS AND MY UNCLE, WHO IS YOUNGER THAN ME AND DECORATE THE TREE. WE DECORATED THAT TREE TO HIGH HEAVENS; ONLY TO PLUG IT UP AND NOTHING. I THOUGHT TO MY TWELVE-YEAR-OLD SELF "THIS NEVER HAPPENS WITH MAMA". FEELING VERY DEFEATED, I NOTIFIED MY SICK MOTHER THAT WE HAD A SURPRISE FOR HER. SHE GOT UP FROM BED, CAME DOWNSTAIRS, & WITH AMAZEMENT SAID "DID YOU ALL CHECK THE BULBS"? THEN IS WHEN I REALIZED; THAT'S RIGHT WE DO CHECK THOSE BULBS EVERY YEAR. I GUESS OUT OF ANTICIPATION & EXCITEMENT I HAD FORGOTTEN TO CHECK THEM. SHE WIGGLED ONE OF THE LOSE BULBS & LIKE MAGIC WE HAD A WELL-LIT BEAUTIFUL

TREE. IN LIFE SOMETIMES PEOPLE PLACES OR THINGS CAN BE YOUR LOSE BULB. DIMMING & DARKENING EVERYTHING YOU DO. THIS CAN COME FROM BELOVED FAMILY MEMBERS & FRIENDS WHO WANT TO COMPETE WITH EVERYTHING YOU DO. PRETENDING TO SUPPORT YOU BUT THE WHOLE TIME WISHING FOR YOUR DOWNFALL. INTIMATE RELATIONSHIPS CAN REALLY DARKEN YOUR PATH ESPECIALLY IF YOU ALL ARE ON TWO DIFFERENT PATHS. THIS WILL BE LIKE THE MIXING OF OIL & WATER; IT JUST WILL NOT WORK! REMEMBER JUST BECAUSE TWO PEOPLE LOVE ONE ANOTHER DOESN'T MEAN THEY ARE COMPATIBLE. VICES WHAT ARE YOUR VICES? THESE ARE THINGS THAT ARE PLEASURABLE TO THE FLESH BUT ARE TOXIC TO YOUR SPIRIT & SOUL THESE THINGS ARE LOSE BULBS TOO. THE MORAL OF THIS STORY IS CHECK YOUR BULBS CONTINUOUSLY & TIGHTEN ANY THAT ARE EVEN REMOTELY (IN THE SLIGHTEST DEGREE) LOSE. THIS WILL CAUSE YOUR LIFE TO BE BRIGHT, POSITIVE, & PRODUCTIVE. LOVE BLACQ

As Property

Can someone explain why people feel they can own a person as property. I mean I always thought once you are delivered from your parents hold you were free to be. Hell most don't even own their home, car, even their shoes are in question. Some folk out here laying away bundles of weave. Then you have the audacity to try and tell another full grown human being what to do. Sorry to be the barrier of this news. a human doesn't belong to you! There is no mortgage company out here with a deed to anyone's ass. Let's get this straight; you can own a dog, fish or pet snake! A human being is a mate to love honor and cherish. Not to be claimed as your property. There is nothing that says you are entitled to a damn thing. Its best if you keep that in mind here going forward cause human beings change like Clark Kent to Superman trying to protect Lois Lane. I'm just saying! In life it is what it is, do

THINGS STRICTLY FROM THE HEART. ANYTHING ELSE WILL LEAVE YOU WONDERING QUESTIONING AND THINKING SOMETHING IS WRONG WITH YOU. LIKE A BUTTERFLY ROAMING FREE SO IS AN INDIVIDUAL HUMAN BEING.

Complicated Things Made Simple

I don't understand why life has to be so complicated. Why do we need to, too, & two? I mean I do understand formal things but the complications of life can be overwhelming. Their & there I know these two words are people & places but why? Know & no pronounced the same but spelled differently; with completely different meanings. Do you sometimes wonder this same thing like why do we need the words read & reed? One thing is for sure we are living in a complicated world with things of the world made even more complicated. One thing you have to do is follow suit in order to become a success! Take a class, commit to a new career, chose reading as a hobby! This is how you make complicated things simple & turn lemons into lemonade.

BLACQ'S TEA

THIS STORY IS A REAL LIFE SITUATIONS MADE INTO A FICTITIOUS TALE, HOWEVER PLEASE BELIEVE THIS CAN HAPPEN ANYWHERE ON EARTH. COLOR, CREED, OR CLASS DOESN'T SAVE YOU FROM. HIS STORY, HER STORY, OR THE UNWANTED.

His Story

He is very deceitful, tall, dark & handsome. Coming from a single parent household where his mom & grand mom literally worshiped him as if he was the second coming! As manipulative as they come this was Only a learned behavior though; something a good ass whipping could have cured! He goes from pillow to post, and since mom has grown tired & grand mom has passed away. He has become the problem of silly women laden. He lies to them and uses sex as his weapon. Any girl's nightmare, disguised as a women's dream come true. He is defiantly counterproductive & has no good idea; fucking & fucking up women's lives is his hobby! He is a red flag walking, cause anyone with good since would recognize the abuse he uses as a part of his deceitful tactics. He is empty, daddy wasn't there! All he knows is excuses; dressed in fine clothes. Clothes he could never afford, but the women who love him will do jail time to prove to him their love. He has

THE TOTAL PACKAGE BETTER KNOWN AS HIV. HE IS AWARE OF THIS FACT WHEN DIAGNOSED THEY TESTED HIM TWICE. HIS IMMUNE SYSTEM IS STRONG, SO HE CARRIES ON AS A HEALTHY BEING LIKE NOTHING AILS HIM AT ALL. HE HAS FATHERED TWELVE CHILDREN ALL BORN HEALTHY AND STRONG, ALTHOUGH THIS MATTERS NOT TO HIM SINCE HE PASSES UNWANTED PACKAGES TO WOMEN AND MOVES RIGHT ALONG. HE HAS NO STABLE ADDRESS ANY OF THE FIFTY STATES COULD BE HIS HOME, FOR THE MOMENT. DON'T ASK TO MANY QUESTIONS OR HE IS GONE. HE HAS BEEN KNOWN TO GET VIOLENT CRUSHING THE NOSES & FACES OF WOMEN INSIDE OF THEIR HOMES. HOMES HE COMES IN TO DESTROY! ALMOST ALWAYS THE WOMEN HE PREYS ON ARE ALREADY BROKEN, DEFEATED, & LEFT ALL ALONE. HE IS ANGRY, HE IS HATE, HE SELF-MEDICATES! THE CYCLE CONTINUES, HE IS THE UNWANTED.

Her Story

She is desirable in many ways. Beautiful, smart, & stacked like a "shit brick house" as the old folks say. See her only problem is she doesn't recognize her beauty. Raised in a two parent household the middle child of six. She has a lot of different complexes. Feelings of being unwanted cause she isn't her families oldest & the baby got all the attention. Stuck smack in the middle looking for love & acceptance in all the wrong places. Fresh out of high school to the stripper pole she strolled. It gave her all the attention she desired and finically; supported her bag addiction down to the very last penny. her addiction didn't stop with purses. no! She was a dope fend anything in a clear plastic bag supported her next high. She isn't considered a prostitute, but Waking up in the arms of strange men was definitely not uncommon for her. The drugs numbed her causing her judgement to leave. She was sick and didn't know it thinking the cough was

JUST THE WEED. SHE HAD HIV. HER LIFESTYLE OF DRINKING, DRUGGING & PROMISCUITY DIDN'T HELP NOT ONE BIT. HER FAMILY COULDN'T SAVE HER EVEN IF THEY TRIED. AS THE BLACK SHEEP SHE WONDERED HOLDING A GRUDGE THAT FOR HER WOULD NEVER EVER DIE.

THE UNWANTED

THEY MEET; IT WAS LUST AT FIRST SIGHT. HE SAW HER SHE WAS THE MOST BEAUTIFUL FEMALE SPECIMEN IN THE ROOM. SHE SMELT HIS COLOGNE AND WAS IN LUST WITH HIS STATURE. LET'S GET A ROOM SO IT CAN GO DOWN; THE WAY IT DOES ON THE MOVIE SCREENS. HAIR PULLING, NECK KISSES, FELLATIO AND CUNNILINGUS. NO MENTIONS OF A CONDOM OR STATUS OF COURSE. BOTH ARE A THREAT TO THEMSELVES AND OTHERS. HURTING AND BROKEN NOT EVEN IN LOVE WITH SELF. TWO THINGS HAPPENED IN THE MIDST OF THIS LUST FILLED, SUPPOSEDLY FUN NIGHT. THE UNWANTED WERE CONCEIVED AND TRANSFERRED. THE UNWANTED ARE TWO, WELL ACTUALLY ONE CAME WITH FRIENDS. THEY KIND OF CLUSTER TOGETHER IN A GROUP. AND THE OTHER IS JUST AN INNOCENT VICTIM OF THE NIGHT'S PLEASURE. THE NIGHT HAS ENDED NO NUMBER EXCHANGE NEEDED. THE THOUGHT DID ENTER HIS MIND THOUGH. HE ACTUALLY LIKED HER, ALTHOUGH HE KNEW IT WAS A WASTE OF TIME. APPARENTLY SHE GETS AROUND AND HE WAS DEFINITELY FAIR GAME. THEY BOTH BELONGED TO ANYONE WILLING TO

TAKE A RISK. WEEKS HAVE PASSED SIX TO BE EXACT. SHE COULD HARDLY DANCE, HER DRUGS HAD BEEN LIMITED TO FEW, THE NAUSEA & VOMITING HAD HER SICK & CONFUSED. SHE DECIDES THAT THIS ILLNESS IS OVERWHELMING; WAY TOO MUCH TO BARE. IT IS MESSING WITH HER COINS & FOR HER THAT WAS UNFAIR. TO THE CLINIC SHE RAN, ABORTIONS AND CURED SEXUALLY TRANSMITTED DESEASES FILLED THE AIR. THE DOCTORS ASK ALL THE TYPICAL QUESTION, & MOVED ON TO THE ROUTINE TESTING. MA'AM CONGRATULATIONS TWO LINES APPEARED; THESE LINES EXPLAIN THE NAUSEA AND VOMITING. STARTLED SHE SAYS "UM OKAY"! SINCE AN ABORTION IS DEFINITELY AN OPTION A CHILD WITH NO FATHER; NO ONE WANTS. MAYBE JUST MAYBE I'LL KEEP IT, I COULD USE A BOUNCING BUNDLE OF JOY. IT COULD LOVE ME LIKE NO OTHER AND MEDICATE MY HEART & MENTAL SORES. SHE LEAVES THE APPOINTMENT FEELING SOME STRANGE NEW WAY, WITH HER FEELING STILL MIXED. AFTER MUCH CONSIDERATION AND TALKING TO A FRIEND SHE DECIDED TO KEEP THE UNNAMED CHILD SHE CARRIED WITHIN. NO NEED TO SEARCH FOR HIM; HE WOULD PROBABLY ONLY DENY IT. SHE STOPPED DANCING & DRUGGING A RESPONSIBLE DECISION ALONG WITH PRENATAL CARE. SHE WAS STILL SUPER TIRED & THE BAGS UNDER HER EYES WERE SCARY

AND DARK. HER FACE WAS DISFIGURED. THE FIRST OB-GYN VISIT COMES; THIS VISIT IS ROUTINE FOR EVERY EXPECTING MOMMY TO BE. URANALYSIS, BLOOD WORK, PAP SMEAR. BABIES HEARTBEAT IS FINE! MA'AM THINGS ARE LOOKING GOOD; DON'T WORRY TOO MUCH ABOUT THE BRUISED SKINNED & FATIGUE THIS IS A PART OF PREGNANCY. HERE ARE SOME PRENATAL VITAMINS TAKE ONE EACH DAY THIS WILL HELP YOUR BABY GROW HEALTHY & STRONG. SHE QUESTIONED THAT THOUGH SHE KNEW A LOT OF PREGNANT GIRLS. SHE GOOGLED HER SYMPTOMS AND FOUND OUT FOR SURE. SO SHE HOPED, SHE WAS SUFFERING FROM A PREGNANCY MASK THIS HAPPENS TO A FEW WHO HAVE A LOW IMMUNE SYSTEM DURING PREGNANCY. RELIEVED SHE CARRIED ON PLANNING AND CHANGING WHERE NECESSARY FOR THE NOW WANTED CHILD THAT WAS ABOUT TO COME INTO HER LIFE. LATER ON THAT WEEK SHE WAS RUSHED TO THE E.R. WITH PELVIC PAINS CRAMPING AND BLOODY SHOW. THE DOCTOR IN THE E.R. GAVE HER THE NEWS. YOU HAVE MISCARRIED DUE TO STD'S IDENTIFIED AS TRICHOMONAS, CHLAMYDIA, & GONORRHEA. MA'AM SORRY FOR YOUR LOST ALTHOUGH THESE ARE THE CURABLE FEW. HE GAVE INSTRUCTIONS OF NO SEXUAL CONTACT UNTIL THE FOLLOW UP VISIT WITH HER REGULAR OBSTETRICIAN. THEY TREATED HER

THERE WITH WHAT IS KNOWN AS A COCKTAIL. NO DNC REQUIRED THE PREGNANCY WAS JUST A FAIL. TWO WEEKS HAVE GONE BY THE BLOOD, DISCHARGE, AND SMELL HAVE PASSED AWAY; ALONG WITH THE THOUGHTS OF MOTHERHOOD THIS MADE HER MORE DEPRESSED & SAD INSIDE. FEELING ISOLATED, ALL ALONE &MORE TIRED THAN BEFORE. TODAY IS THE FOLLOW UP VISIT WITH HER DOCTOR. SHE SAT AND WAITED FOR HER NAME TO BE CALLED WITH HOPES OF FEELING BETTER MENTALLY, EMOTIONALLY, & PHYSICALLY. NEEDLESS TO SAY SHE DROPPED THE NEWS, "DOCTOR I MISCARRIED NO NEED TO CHECK THE PREVIOUSLY UNWANTED IS GONE" SAD TO SAY THIS, LEAVING OUT ONE LITTLE BIT; THE OTHER UNWANTED GONE ALSO. NO NEED FOR FURTHER EMBARRASSMENT ILL JUST KEEP THAT TO MYSELF AND HEAD HOME. MA'AM BEFORE YOU GO WE MUST GO OVER YOUR TEST RESULTS. SHE REPLY'S "I KNOW; I KNOW"! "I HAD THREE STD'S WHICH CAUSED THE MISCARRIAGE I'VE BEEN TREATED I'M FINE"! "CAN I GO NOW"? MA'AM PLEASE HAVE A SEAT I'LL BE BACK IN A MOMENT. THE DOCTOR COMES BACK WITH A COUNSELOR & SAYS YOU'VE TESTED POSITIVE FOR SYPHILIS & FULL BLOWN AIDS. WE CAN TREAT THE SYPHILIS SINCE IT'S IN THE FIRST STAGE. NOW THE AIDS "WAIT YOU MEAN, HIV RIGHT"? I'M SORRY MA'AM YOUR T-CELL COUNT

SHOULD BE IN THE THOUSANDS YOU'RE NOT EVEN AT TEN. THERE IS NOTHING WE CAN DO AND WE NEED TO TEST YOUR PARTNER TOO. THE UNWANTED HUNTED HER FOR THE LAST OF HER DAYS. AT 25 HER LIFE EXPIRED! THERE WAS NOTHING ANYONE COULD DO. NOT EVEN PRAYER COULD CHANGE HER FATE. A MONTH AFTER HER DEATH HE WENT TO LOOK FOR HER IT WAS SOMETHING ABOUT HER SWAY AND THE WAY SHE DID HER THANG THAT DAY. HE WANTED MORE OF HER, HE SHOWED UP TO THE CLUB KNOWING SHE WOULD BE THERE, BUT WHAT HE FOUND WAS A MEMORIAL AT THE FRONT ENTRANCE THAT SHOWED HER ONCE BEAUTIFUL FACE & IT READ: R.I.P

LARANDA WHO DIED OF FULL BLOWN AIDS. HE CHUCKLED INSIDE THINKING DAMN THAT WAS QUICK! NOT KNOWING HIS STATUS ONLY SPEED UP HER PROCESS. SHE ALREADY HAD THE PACKAGE, SHE WAS ALREADY SICK. HE WALKED AWAY REMORSELESS THINKING ABOUT HOW SILLY WOMEN REALLY ARE. FEELING LIKE ANYONE WHO WHORES AROUND DESERVES JUST WHAT THEY GET. SOMEONE GAVE IT TO HIM WHILE HE WAS IN HIS YOUTH; SIXTEEN TO BE EXACT & SHE WAS THIRTY-TWO. IN HIS MIND HE WAS INNOCENT & WASN'T RESPONSIBLE TO PUT HIS BUSINESS ON BLAST. WHAT HE DIDN'T KNOW WAS

THAT ON THAT PARTICULAR NIGHT HE WAS MESSING WITH SOMEONE JUST AS DANGEROUS AS HE. HER STATUS AFFECTED HIM SEVERELY, THE JOKE WAS ON HIM. AFTER ABOUT TWO WEEKS HE DIED ON THE SIDE OF THE ROAD. BODY MAULED BY ANIMALS HE WAS HITCH HIKING TO CHICAGO, SO HE THOUGHT. IT WAS A HORRIBLE DEATH HE DIED ALL ALONE. TILL THIS DAY HIS MOTHER CAN'T FIND HIM. SHE KNOWS HE IS DEAD! SHE WOULD PAY MONEY FOR HIS BODY. THAT WAS HER ONLY SON. THE WOMEN BEFORE WHERE HEALTHY BEFORE HE GAVE THEM HIV. THEY WERE PRESCRIBED THE APPROPRIATE MEDICATIONS EVEN THE CHILDREN WERE FINE. NOT ONE OF THE UNWANTED TWELVE TESTED POSITIVE GOING ON TO LIVE HEALTHY LIVES. HE NEVER KNEW ANY OF THE CHILDREN. NEITHER DID HIS MOTHER, SO SHE DOESN'T EVEN HAVE GRANDCHILDREN TO COMFORT HER. THAT ONE WOMEN, THAT ONE DAY ENDED HIS LIFE. AT THE RIPE AGE OF 28 HIS STATUS WAS POSITIVE AND HIS POLICY WAS DON'T ASK DON'T TELL.

IN CLOSING, REMEMBER LOOKS CAN BE DECEITFUL, NEITHER OF THE CHARACTERS "LOOKED" AS IF THEY LIVED SUCH DANGEROUS LIFESTYLES. WHEN INVOLVING YOUR LIFE WITH STRANGERS ASK QUESTIONS. MAKE IT A RULE TO SPEND TIME IN CONVERSATION ABOUT

PERSONAL THINGS. LOOKS CAN BE VERY DECEITFUL. RATHER MALE OR FEMALE YOUR BODY IS A PRECIOUS VESSEL. THIS VESSEL THAT WE HAVE BEEN BLESSED WITH, CAN BE FILLED WITH BOTH NEGATIVE AND POSITIVE THINGS. WHAT THINGS WILL YOU ALLOW YOUR VESSEL TO BE FILLED WITH? IT'S YOUR PURGATIVE TO KNOW WHEN THE LAST TIME; IF EVER YOUR SEXUAL PARTNER WAS TESTED. IF SOMEONE FEELS THEY ARE WORTHY OF YOUR VESSEL THEY WILL BE WILLING TO GO GET TESTED WITH YOU. IF THEY FEEL THAT'S TOO MUCH, THEN GUESS WHAT? MAYBE THEY ARE HIDING SOMETHING. SOMEONE WORTHY OF YOU WILL BE LIMITLESSLY OPEN TO ANYTHING YOU DEEM NECESSARY BEFORE YOU SHARE THAT PART OF YOU WITH THEM. I HAVE PUT TOGETHER A FEW RULES TO FOLLOW IN DATING THAT MAY HELP YOU RATIONALIZE AND THINK BEFORE YOU PLACE YOURSELF IN DANGEROUS SEXUAL RELATIONSHIPS.

1. ASK ALL NECESSARY QUESTIONS.

2. BE OPEN AND HONEST ABOUT YOUR SEXUAL DEALINGS & ENCOURAGE THE SAME.

3. PLAN THE FIRST SEXUAL ENCOUNTER WITH A VISIT TO YOUR LOCAL CLINIC.

4. USE PROTECTION. THIS WILL CUT DOWN YOUR RISK FOR SEXUALLY TRANSMITTED DISEASES & CHILDREN NO ONE WANTS.

5. LASTLY, LOVE YOURSELF ENOUGH TO BE & STAY HEALTHY. YOU ARE WORTH THE TEST IT TAKES TO PROVE YOUR PARTNER'S HEALTH, & TO ENSURE YOURS.

KNOW YOUR STATUS, GET TESTED!

BLACQ'S COGNAC

I HAVE TWO

TRUTH IS I AM INTENSELY IN LOVE WITH TWO. BEFORE I DIVULGE THIS TEA UNDERSTAND THIS; I AM BEYOND STATUS QUO. NORMALITY FOR ME IS PLACED ON THE TOP SELF WITH HOW I FEEL ABOUT YOUR JUDGEMENT. THE DESCRIPTION OF MY SUITOR IS SIMPLE; HE IS THE ANGEL ON THE RIGHT SHOULDER WITH LOVE LIKE THE SANDS OF ALL SEVEN SEAS. HAPPY KNOWING, HE IS RIGHT NEXT TO ME. EVEN THOUGH HE IS ANY WOMAN'S DREAM, THAT VICE THAT RIPS ME LIKE FLESH FROM THE BONE TORN ON A BOB WIRE FENCE, IS MY INAMORATA. HE IS THE DEVIL SO SLY AND CUNNING LINGERING IN THE SHADOWS TO THE LEFT WITH HIS PHALLUS! HE IS SO IN LUST WITH MY WALK, TALK, AND WAY OF DRESS, MY LIPS, HIPS & FINGER TIPS. IT'S HARD FOR ME TO RESIST THE BECKONING OF THE BEST LOVER I'VE KNOWN SO WHEN HE CALLS I'M DRIFTED BY THE SMELL OF HIS EXPENSIVE COLOGNE. NOT TO A GOOD PLACE THOUGH, THERE WITH HIM LIES DECEIT, MALICE AND CONTINUOUSLY DRIED TEARS. TEARS DRIED BY MY FUTURE CONSORT FROM THE DAY WE MEET. YOU SEE MY LOVER WAS ONCE MY FRIEND BUT

NOT REALLY. HE WAS CRAFTY IN HIS DELIVERY BUT THE MOMENT I LET DOWN MY GUARDS HE POUNCED LIKE A LIONESS ON THE HUNT. ONLY TO ATTACH HIMSELF TO EVERY OPPORTUNITY I HAD AVAILABLE AND COME AND GO AS A SHIFTLESS SOUL. CONNECTED ONLY FOR WHATEVER HE COULD GET; MAINLY SEX. LIKE A FOOLISH SCHOOL GIRL, I FEEL IN LOVE WITH HIS POTENTIAL. THE WHOLE WHILE HE WAS LOOKING, SEARCHING FOR HIS NEXT VICTIM. BORED WITH MY COMPASSION AND GENUINE LOVE. THE OPPORTUNITY TO SAY "I DO" HAS COME. I ACCEPT WITH UNDERSTANDING THAT A POLYAMOROUS SOUL NEEDS MORE THAN ONE. I'M TRAPPED WITH MIND CONTROL & THOUGHTS OF THE NEXT ORGASMIC HIGH. HAPPILY, WEDDED I'LL CONTINUE MY ESCAPADES HOPING TO FIND THE FORMULA TO MAKE MY LUST FOR THIS HORRID VICE MEET ITS DEMISE.

Pussy Power

The shit I'm about to say may seem vulgar, but I just have to keep shit real! Pussy power is an unrecognized beast mainly unrecognized by its possessors, women. Take heed ladies this game I'm about to spit goes deep! That thang in-between your legs makes life sweet! It is lady like, it self-cleans & if a smell amerces please go see the local gyn. Take care of it & in turn it will take care of you. Busting wide open the nose of a potential bow. he doesn't even have to touch it just the anticipation & wait makes him do everything he can to obtain your forbidden fruit. Pay attention ladies, since attached to this lesson are a few rules. Drink plenty of lemon water and stay in your lane. This help the ph. & keeps pissy, fishy smells away. Have a yearly pap smear stay on top

OF YOUR GAME. UTERINE CANCER IS EASIEST TO CURE BUT IF YOU DON'T KNOW, IT WON'T SHOW UNTIL YOUR FAMILY IS BURYING YOU. WITH THAT THANG YOU CAN'T BE TO LOSE SINCE THAT ISN'T TO SAFE & DEFINITELY GOES AGAINST THE RULES. ALWAYS USE PROTECTION NO MATTER WHO IT IS WITH THERE ARE SO MANY WAYS THAT IT CAN GET SICK. WITH THAT BEING SAID LET'S ADMIT PUSSY RULES. THE PRECIOUS JEWEL THAT WE WOMEN POSSESS CAN BE USED FOR A GOOD OR EVIL TOOL. WOMEN COMPLAIN ABOUT MEN AND THEIR SNEAKY LYING WAYS. HOWEVER, TODAY LET'S SET THE RECORD STRAIGHT. WOMEN LIE, CHEAT, & SCHEME JUST AS MUCH & MORE THAN MEN DO. THEY JUST DON'T GET CAUGHT BECAUSE PUSSY WILL HAVE AH NIGGA LOOKING LIKE A STRAIGHT FOOL. WHILE SHE FUCKING HIS HOMIES, MAYBE HIS BROTHER TOO. HER LIPS, HIPS, & FINGER TIPS SEDUCE HIM & HER WORD BECOMES MORE THAN A SUNDAY SCHOOL PRAYER BOOK. PUSSY HAS THE POWER TO GET A FOOL KILLED. SO UNLESS YOU WANT STAINED BLOOD ON YOUR HANDS BE HONEST AND TRUE. ON THE FLIP SIDE OF THIS THING, PUSSY CAN BE MORE TO A MAN THAN HIS VERY BEST FRIEND. BARING CHILDREN THAT WILL CARRY HIS LAST NAME & PLEASURE ON HIS MARITAL BED. WHAT I AM SAYING IS SOME EASY BOTTOM SHELF SO THE KIDDIES CAN READ IT TYPE SHIT. HOWEVER

YOU CHOOSE TO USE IT KNOW THIS! PUSSY POWER IS GREATER THAN THE AIR AH NIGGA BREATHS. I KNOW YOU THINKING HOW DOES SHE KNOW THIS? HELL, I ASKED HE REPLIED & I STARTED TO TYPE. I TYPED WHAT HE SAID VERBATIM NOT LEAVING OUT ONE WORD. HE SAID "BABY NIGGAS BUILT A WHOLE CIVILIZATION FOR PUSSY" IT'S A REAL MAN'S MOJO IT GIVES HIM HIS STRIDE! MY MAN PRETTY SMART SO I WAS COMPELLED TO SHARE THIS WITH YOU. PUSSY POWER IS YOUR KEY LADIES BUT, YOU MUST USE IT WISELY.

Sur-real Nigga Shit

The state of being so unreal its bizarre, unreal, uncanny, Ha you must be dreaming. Real nigga is what they calling it now? A full grown man that hasn't matured past adolescence. Pants sagging, cellphone in tote ready to pop game to whomever is willing to listen. Swaged down but with that same phone refuse to dial children you took full responsibility to create. I mean we don't have to state exactly what took place, but when the delivery date was mentioned you said we will wait to see if that child I have to mention! The rejection from the womb and we wonder why this viscous cycle continues. Hell my daddy sold a dream and created fiend's out of women; multiples. Real nigga you say? In all actuality you as fake as a three-dollar bill counterfeit not to be trusted. Living pillow to post becoming a ghost the figment of another women's imagination. Saying you are a real nigga is just proof, that you don't know your worth or pure truth; truth of the King that

44

LIES WITHIN AND THE NATION THAT YOU COULD HELP REBUILD! REAL NIGGA ARE WORDS THAT HAVE NO NEED FOR UTTERANCE, ESPECIALLY SINCE WORDS ARE DEAD. ACTIONS BRING WORDS TO LIFE ARE YOU CAPABLE TO ACT OUT TRUTH? PROBABLY NOT! QUITE FRANKLY I NEED ANSWERS PLEASE. HOW REAL CAN YOU BE WHEN YOUR AGE RANGE SPEAKS VOLUMES TO YOUR LEGACY, YOU HAVE NO EARTHLY POSSESSION NOT EVEN AN APARTMENT KEY. REAL NIGGA YOU DO REALIZE RAPPERS ARE ENTERTAINERS, RIGHT? MOST HAVE COLLEGE DEGREES. REAL NIGGAS I LAUGH SO HARD BECAUSE WHAT'S SO REAL ABOUT A MAN THAT CHATTERS LIKE A CACKLE OF HENS? PLEASE SPARE ME. REAL NIGGA YOU DO KNOW THOSE JAY'S YOU JUST PURCHASED COST MAYBE THIRTEEN DOLLARS TO MAKE AND CAN'T FEED NOR CLOTH YOU FOR GOODNESS SAKE. ONE LAST THING THE NEXT TIME YOU COMMIT A CRIME PLEASE BY ALL MEANS DO THE TIME LIKE A REAL NIGGA SHOULD; WITHOUT CALLING DRIVING EVERY DAMN BODIES PHONE BILLS UP. NOW THAT'S ONE-HUNDRED PERCENT REAL, NIGGA.

A Raw Game

RED, PAINFUL AS THE RESULT OF AN ABRASION. HOW IS IT THAT SOMETHING SO UNPLEASANT CAN COME FROM LOVE? I MEAN AT LEAST; THAT'S WHAT IT WAS FOR ME. UNTIL; YOU BROUGHT THE PAINS OF TEN THOUSAND TORTURE CHAMBERS, YOUR TRUTH. MY BREATH STOPPED AND TIME FROZE. MY HEART BURNED WITH THE PASSIONS OF MY WASTED TIME, IT WAS RAW REALLY SORE. I DECIDED TO ALLOW YOU INTO MY HEART, MY SACRED PLACE A PLACE WHERE NO MAN HAD EVER TRAVELED AND MAYBE, JUST MAYBE NO OTHER WILL. MY HEART WAS YOUR MARTYR CRUCIFIED BECAUSE OF ITS CHOICE TO LOVE YOU. AGONIZED BY THE MOMENTS SNATCHED AWAY WITH NO WARNING, NO CLOSURE DAMN! THE REALITY OF IT ALL WAS LIE'S, DECEIT, AND OPPORTUNITY FOR YOU. CAN I BLAME YOU? NO NOT REALLY I WAS EASY PREY. GULLIBLE, GREEN, SUFFERING FROM THE DADDY SYNDROME. ACCORDING TO MY GRANDMOTHER IT'S ALL IN THE RAISING, WELL WE WERE DEFINITELY RAISED DIFFERENTLY! WHERE I COME FROM A PERSON LIKE YOU IS CONSIDERED AS "ONE WHO PLAYS THE

GAME RAW". NO GOOD END COMES TO THIS TYPE OF INDIVIDUAL THEY USUALLY END UP DEAD, IN JAIL OR JUST ALL ALONE. I DON'T WISH THIS FATE ON ANY PERSON, FOR I AM A GENUINE LOVER. ALTHOUGH IT'S A FACT THAT THE DIVIDER BETWEEN LOVE AND HATE IS AS FINE AS A STRAND OF HAIR AND EVEN THAT IS A LITTLE THICK FOR THIS DESCRIPTION. MY HEART IS SORE IN PLACES I NEVER KNEW EXISTED. I MUST ADMIT I THOUGHT ABOUT CALLING HOME AND HAVING MY BROTHERS COME HANDLE SOME SHIT. I THOUGHT ABOUT SHOWING UP UNANNOUNCED BUSTING OUT THE WINDOWS TO YOUR CAR AND HOUSE. NO, THAT ISN'T IT! YOUR JOB WAS IN JEOPARDY AS WELL AS YOUR LIFE. MOMMA DIDN'T RAISE NO DAMN FOOL THOUGH, PLUS I HAVE WAY TOO MUCH CLASS FOR ALL THAT. SO I SAT TO MYSELF FELT THE PAIN, CRIED THE TEARS, REMINISCED AND THOUGHT ABOUT ALL THE TIMES I GAVE YOU ME. EVERY OUNCE OF ME WITHOUT HESITATION AND YOU TOOK IT ALL. MY DECISION TODAY IS ALLOWING MY HEART TO HEAL, FORGIVE YOU AS WELL AS FORGIVE MYSELF, AND LOVE MY HEART BACK TO ITS PLACE OF SERENITY, BEFORE I ALLOWED YOU TO MAKE IT RAW. WE WERE BOTH TO BLAME.

With Him

With him came the freedom of ten-thousand freed slaves. All the inhibitions left causing my love life to change. Free from debt of lover's before. With him I felt a tingle in my spine and butterflies even after the first time. With him I feel insecure though, somehow I'm not good enough for him. With him my spirit calls out to his for truth, truth that could take this to a plane not imaginable with a human mind. With him he doesn't communicate; with each kiss, each touch, each moan and every toe curl. I should know. With him the farther we go the harder it seems to be real. In my emotion it feels as if we been we for ten thousand years. With him it's only a waste of time cause his wall is as callused skin. With him has left my desire to love ever again. With him my love stood still.

SEDATION

GOOD DICK ATTACHED TO A FINE MALE SPECIMEN. HIS STROLL IS CHARISMATICALLY SICK THE PLEASURE I RECEIVE FROM HIM TRUMPS THE RICHTER. HE IS MY GO TO AFTER A LONG DAY MY INSPIRATION TO BE HIS STRIPPER HIS WHORE. MY BODY IS HIS DOMAIN. ALLOWING HIM TO UTILIZE EVERY HOLE WITH HIS MAGIC POLE TOGETHER WE CREATE A WHOLE UNIVERSE BIGGER THAN THE MILKY WAY IN ITS ENTIRETY; I KNOW HIM HE KNOWS ME. AS I REVERSE COWBOY MOMENTS LATER A 69 TAKES PLACE; NOT A LOT OF WORK INVOLVED THOUGH, ONE KISS TO HIS MANDINGO MAN STICK & IT'S AT FULL ATTENTION BECAUSE THEY KNOW WHAT THEY ARE ABOUT TO GET. DEEP THROAT, BALLS LICKED, KISSED, SUCKED, TITTY FUCKED. SHOVED DOWN MY THROAT UNTIL IT CUMS! THEN IT RISES AGAIN & I OBLIGE SINCE I'M A TEAM PLAYER. THEN I THROW MY ASS IN THE AIR & ARCH MY BACK HE LOVES THAT. I CUM EVERYWHERE ALL ON HIM, HIS STOMACH. WE ARE PLEASED, I LOVE TO BE HIS FREAK IN THE SHEETS. FULLY SEDATED WE LAY.

Phallus Head

Undeniable passion, rubbing, touching, kissing, & fucking you! I absolutely lust everything about you. Your structure your style, the way you look dress & smell. Damn! Wait there is one small problem; so does every woman. Every woman lusts you, they wish oh how they wish they were in my shoes. Being with you exchanging fuck faces, grabbing, tugging & lusting with you! Only if they knew something is horribly missing. A woman is valueless to you, worth only one thing a good screw! This is a story about a phallus head & man's true best friend. Erected it can bring life to a woman in several ways. Her breath leaves her being as It enters her middle space. Creating an orgasmic feeling sometimes unexplained. This extension to the male body is such a beautiful thing. With his dick a man can completely rule a house hold causing his woman to be a humble as a lamb. Cooking, cleaning, baring his children & his name forsaking all others.

A PHALLUS HEAD GIVEN TO A WOMAN BY THE WRONG MAN CAN HAVE AH BITCH STRUNG OUT LIKE SHE ON THAT DOPE, PROSTITUTING HER SELF-RAIN SLEET OR SNOW. THAT SHIT CAN GO SO DEEP THAT THE RIGHT PHALLUS HEAD ENTRY WILL HAVE YOU CUSSING OUT YOUR MOTHER! LIKE FUCK THIS SHIT I'M GROWN & I LOVE HIM! SHE WILL SIMPLY REPLY IF YOU LOVE HIM YOU LOVE NOTHING, BUT YOU WON'T GIVE A DAMN! YOU KNOW I AIN'T LYING. SITTING THERE LOOKING CRAZY ISOLATED AWAY FROM FAMILY & FRIENDS, MEANWHILE HIS MOTHER LIVING IN YOUR DEN. THE MORAL OF THIS STORY IS IT'S NOT WORTH IT. IF THE PHALLUS HEAD IS NOT ATTACHED TO A REAL KING WHO WON'T USE IT TO ABUSE YOU; LEAVE IT ALONE IT WILL SUCK YOU DRY LIKE GRAPES PURPOSELY LEFT IN THE SUN TO MAKE RAISINS!

SIDE HOE

WE ARE FRIENDS, HOW CAN YOU DO THIS? I TRUSTED
YOU WITH MY KIDS THEIR FATHER YOU FUCKED!
REALLY? HOW COULD YOU CHOOSE TO BUST A NUT
OVER A FRIENDSHIP WE'VE MAINTAINED SINCE THE
FIFTH GRADE? MY SISTER, THE GODMOTHER OF OUR
CHILDREN NOW BECOMES MY KID'S SIBLINGS MOTHER,
SINCE YOU ALL CHOSE NOT TO USE A RUBBER! I BLAME
YOU! HERE WITH ME HE REMAINS BECAUSE HE LOVES
ME YOU SEE! HOW SILLY CAN YOU BE YOU THOUGHT
HE WOULD LEAVE ME FOR YOU? MAYBE YOU BELIEVED
HE WOULD TREAT YOU THE WAY HE TREATS ME & THIS
BASTARD YOU CARRY WOULD MAKE HIS EYES GLEAM
AS MY CHILDREN DO. NOT SURE WHAT YOU TRIED TO
ACCOMPLISH BEING THE SIDE DISH I GUESS. EITHER
WAY IT GOES I WILL FIGHT YOU & AN ARMY OF YOUR
KIND FOR MY MAN! ONCE MY COMPANION TURNED
SIDE HOE! I'M TITLED HIS MAIN CHICK WHILE EVEN
IF HE STILL FUCKS YOU DICK IS ALL YOU WILL GET! WE
HAVE PLAYED HOUSE FOR TEN YEARS, WE HAVE THREE
KIDS, THIS SECURES MY SPOT AT THE ALTER WHEN HE
IS READY. THIS PROVES HE LOVES ME SO I'LL WAIT.

SINCE BIBLE TIMES WOMEN ARE BLAMED FOR SLEEPING WITH MEN WHO ARE SUPPOSEDLY COMMITTED TO OTHER WOMEN, WHILE THE MAN GOES ON WITH NO RESPONSIBILITY WHAT-SO-EVER! I ABSOLUTELY DESPISE THIS! NOW DAYS THEY ARE BEING CALLED SIDE HOE'S. THIS IS UTTERLY RIDICULOUS. IN FACT, IF YOUR MAN IS ACTIVELY SLEEPING WITH ANOTHER WOMAN/WOMEN HE IS IN RELATIONSHIP WITH THEM & THIS MAKES EVERY LAST ONE OF YOU GIRLFRIENDS HOPING TO BE CHOSE. IF YOU STAY WITH A MAN THAT IS WILLING TO PLACE YOU IN THE POSITION OF BEING CONFRONTED BY ANOTHER WOMAN/WOMEN, OR EVEN HAVING TO BARE THE PAIN OF SHARING HIM WITH HER & OTHER CHILDREN, YOU ARE SETTLING & CAN ONLY BLAME YOURSELF. IF THERE ARE TEXT SHE ISN'T TEXTING HERSELF, IF THEY HAD SEX SHE DIDN'T FUCK HERSELF, IF THERE IS A CHILD SHE DEFINITELY DIDN'T GET HERSELF PREGNANT! PLEASE IF YOU ARE IN A RELATIONSHIP WITH A JIG-ALOO & YOU EXCEPT HIM & CHILDREN HE MADE DURING THE DURATION OF YOUR TIME WITH HIM GO AHEAD & ACCEPT YOUR STABLE SISTERS & PLEASE STOP CALLING THEM SIDE HOES CAUSE THAT'S JUST PLAIN NASTY & RUDE.

BLACQ'S PRELUDE
TO THE LOVE OF WORD'S

THE LOVE OF WORDS

I AM ADDICTED TO A SUBSTANCE, NOT JUST ANY SUBSTANCE, NO! ONE THAT STANDS ALONE WITH SPACE ON EITHER SIDE. THIS LOVE WITHIN ME IS NOT NECESSARILY RARE NO! I'M CONFIDENT THAT THERE ARE OTHERS LIKE ME, MAYBE YOU ARE ADDICTED JUST THE SAME. NO MATTER HOW I'VE TRIED I CAN'T SEEM TO ESCAPE THE GRASP OF THIS THING IT HAS A TIGHT HOLD OF ME. FROM A YOUNG GIRL IT HAS HAUNTED ME; CAUSING MY CURIOSITIES TO ARISE MORE AND MORE AFTER EACH HIGH. THIS STORY WILL EXPOSE MY ADDICTION LAYING MYSELF COMPLETELY BARE WHILE RAISING AWARENESS OF THE DISEASE IN WHICH I SUFFER. I AM A LOGOPHILLIAC AND THESE ARE MY CONFESSIONS. ENTER WITH CAUTION IF NOT ALREADY; YOU TOO MAY LEAVE ADDICTED

Printed in the United States
By Bookmasters